Cram101 Textbook Outlines to accompany:

Strategic Management and Competitive Advantage : Concepts and Cases

William Hesterly, 1st Edition

A Content Technologies Inc. publication (c) 2012.

Cram101 Textbook Outlines and Cram101.com are Cram101 Inc. publications and services. All notes, highlights, reviews, and practice tests are written and prepared by Content Technologies and Cram101, all rights reserved.

STUDYING MADE EASY

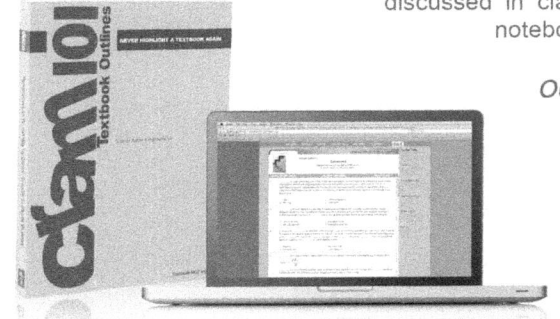

This Cram101 notebook is designed to make studying easier and increase your comprehension of the textbook material. Instead of starting with a blank notebook and trying to write down everything discussed in class lectures, you can use this Cram101 textbook notebook and annotate your notes along with the lecture.

Our goal is to give you the best tools for success.

For a supreme understanding of the course, pair your notebook with our online tools. Should you decide you prefer Cram101.com as your study tool,

we'd like to offer you a trade...

Our Trade In program is a simple way for us to keep our promise and provide you the best studying tools, regardless of where you purchased your Cram101 textbook notebook. As long as your notebook is in *Like New Condition**, you can send it back to us and we will immediately give you a Cram101.com account free for 120 days!

Let The **Trade In** Begin!

THREE SIMPLE STEPS TO TRADE:

1. Go to www.cram101.com/tradein and fill out the packing slip information.
2. Submit and print the packing slip and mail it in with your Cram101 textbook notebook.
3. Activate your account after you receive your email confirmation.

* Books must be returned in *Like New Condition*, meaning there is no damage to the book including, but not limited to; ripped or torn pages, markings or writing on pages, or folded / creased pages. Upon receiving the book, Cram101 will inspect it and reserves the right to terminate your free Cram101.com account and return your textbook notebook at the owners expense.

Learning System

Cram101 Textbook Outlines is a learning system. The notes in this book are the highlights of your textbook, you will never have to highlight a book again.

How to use this book. Take this book to class, it is your notebook for the lecture. The notes and highlights on the left hand side of the pages follow the outline and order of the textbook. All you have to do is follow along while your instructor presents the lecture. Circle the items emphasized in class and add other important information on the right side. With Cram101 Textbook Outlines you'll spend less time writing and more time listening. Learning becomes more efficient.

Cram101.com Online

Increase your studying efficiency by using Cram101.com's practice tests and online reference material. It is the perfect complement to Cram101 Textbook Outlines. Use self-teaching matching tests or simulate in-class testing with comprehensive multiple choice tests, or simply use Cram's true and false tests for quick review. Cram101.com even allows you to enter your in-class notes for an integrated studying format combining the textbook notes with your class notes.

Visit **www.Cram101.com**, click Sign Up at the top of the screen, and enter **DK73DW14952** in the promo code box on the registration screen. Your access to www.Cram101.com is discounted by 50% because you have purchased this book. Sign up and stop highlighting textbooks forever.

Copyright © 2011 by Cram101, Inc. All rights reserved. "Cram101"® and "Never Highlight a Book Again!"® are registered trademarks of Cram101, Inc. ISBN(s): 9781428845619. PUBE-1.2011830

Strategic Management and Competitive Advantage : Concepts and Cases
William Hesterly, 1st

CONTENTS

1. What Is Strategy and the Strategic Management Process? 2
2. Evaluating a Firm's External Environment 18
3. Evaluating a Firm's Internal Capabilities 38
4. Cost Leadership 46
5. Product Differentiation 56
6. Vertical Integration 68
7. Corporate Diversification 76
8. Organizing to Implement Corporate Diversification 84
9. Strategic Alliances 96

Chapter 1. What Is Strategy and the Strategic Management Process?

Strategic management	Strategic management is a field that deals with the major intended and emergent initiatives taken by general managers on behalf of owners, involving utilization of resources, to enhance the performance of ?rms in their external environments. It entails specifying the organization's mission, vision and objectives, developing policies and plans, often in terms of projects and programs, which are designed to achieve these objectives, and then allocating resources to implement the policies and plans, projects and programs. A balanced scorecard is often used to evaluate the overall performance of the business and its progress towards objectives.
Management process	Management process is a process of planning and controlling the performance or execution of any type of activity, such as: • a project (project management process) or • a process (process management process is responsible for carrying out its management process. However, this is not always the case for all management processes, for example, it is the responsibility of the project manager to carry out a project management process.
Mission statement	A mission statement is a formal, short, written statement of the purpose of a company or organization. The mission statement should guide the actions of the organization, spell out its overall goal, provide a sense of direction, and guide decision-making. It provides 'the framework or context within which the company's strategies are formulated.' Historically it is associated with Christian religious groups; indeed, for many years, a missionary was assumed to be a person on a specifically religious mission.
Policy	A policy is typically described as a principle or rule to guide decisions and achieve rational outcome(s). The term is not normally used to denote what is actually done, this is normally referred to as either procedure or protocol. Whereas a policy will contain the 'what' and the 'why', procedures or protocols contain the 'what', the 'how', the 'where', and the 'when'.
Cost leadership	Cost leadership is a concept developed by Michael Porter, used in business strategy. It describes a way to establish the competitive advantage. Cost leadership, in basic words, means the lowest cost of operation in the industry.
Diversification	In finance, diversification means reducing risk by investing in a variety of assets. If the asset values do not move up and down in perfect synchrony, a diversified portfolio will have less risk than the weighted average risk of its constituent assets, and often less risk than the least risky of its constituents.. Therefore, any risk-averse investor will diversify to at least some extent, with more risk-averse investors diversifying more completely than less risk-averse investors.

Chapter 1. What Is Strategy and the Strategic Management Process?

Chapter 1. What Is Strategy and the Strategic Management Process?

Management control system	A management control systems is a system which gathers and uses information to evaluate the performance of different organizational resources like human, physical, financial and also the organization as a whole considering the organizational strategies. Finally, Management control system influences the behavior of organizational resources to implement organizational strategies. Management control system might be formal or informal.
Organizational structure	An organizational structure consists of activities such as task allocation, coordination and supervision, which are directed towards the achievement of organizational aims. It can also be considered as the viewing glass or perspective through which individuals see their organization and its environment. Many organizations have hierarchical structures, but not all.
Product	The noun product is defined as a 'thing produced by labor or effort' or the 'result of an act or a process', and stems from the verb produce, from the Latin produce(re) '(to) lead or bring forth'. Since 1575, the word 'product' has referred to anything produced. Since 1695, the word has referred to 'thing or things produced'.
Product differentiation	In economics and marketing, product differentiation is the process of distinguishing a product or offering from others, to make it more attractive to a particular target market. This involves differentiating it from competitors' products as well as a firm's own product offerings. The concept was proposed by Edward Chamberlin in his 1933 Theory of Monopolistic Competition.
Vertical integration	In microeconomics and management, the term vertical integration describes a style of management control. Vertically integrated companies in a supply chain are united through a common owner. Usually each member of the supply chain produces a different product or (market-specific) service, and the products combine to satisfy a common need.
Leadership	Leadership has been described as the 'process of social influence in which one person can enlist the aid and support of others in the accomplishment of a common task'. Definitions more inclusive of followers have also emerged. Alan Keith of Genentech states that, 'Leadership is ultimately about creating a way for people to contribute to making something extraordinary happen.' According to Ken 'SKC' Ogbonnia, 'effective leadership is the ability to successfully integrate and maximize available resources within the internal and external environment for the attainment of organizational or societal goals.'

Chapter 1. What Is Strategy and the Strategic Management Process?

Chapter 1. What Is Strategy and the Strategic Management Process?

	The following sections discuss several important aspects of leadership including a description of what leadership is and a description of several popular theories and styles of leadership.
Competitive advantage	Competitive advantage is defined as the strategic advantage one business entity has over its rival entities within its competitive industry. Achieving competitive advantage strengthens and positions a business better within the business environment. Resource-based view perspective Competitive advantage is a theory that seeks to address some of the criticisms of comparative advantage.
Standard accounting practice	Standard accounting practices require publicly-traded companies to follow certain accounting rules when presenting financial statements so that the readers of the statements can easily compare different companies. Private companies are also often required by banks and shareholders, for example, to present information according to their specified rules. Usually, countries practicing civil law system write standards into law and countries with English common law systems have private organizations to set the rules.
LIFO	LIFO is an acronym which stands for last in, first out. In computer science and queueing theory this refers to the way items stored in some types of data structures are processed. By definition, in a LIFO structured linear list, elements can be added or taken off from only one end, called the 'top'.
Leverage	In negotiation, leverage is the ability to influence the other side to move closer to one's negotiating position.

Chapter 1. What Is Strategy and the Strategic Management Process?

Chapter 1. What Is Strategy and the Strategic Management Process?

	Types of leverage include positive leverage, negative leverage, and normative leverage. Normative Leverage Normative leverage is the application of general norms or the other party's standards and norms to advance one's own arguments for one's own good.
Accounts receivable	Accounts receivable, is money owed to a business by its clients (customers) and shown on its Balance Sheet as an asset. It is one of a series of accounting transactions dealing with the billing of a customer for goods and services that the customer has ordered. Overview Accounts receivable represent money owed by entities to the firm on the sale of products or services on credit.
Cash flow	Cash flow is the movement of cash into or out of a business, project, or financial product. (Note that 'cash' is used here in the broader sense of the term, where it includes bank deposits). It is usually measured during a specified, finite period of time.
Earnings per share	Earnings per share is the amount of earnings per each outstanding share of a company's stock. In the United States, the Financial Accounting Standards Board (FASB) requires companies' income statements to report Earnings per share for each of the major categories of the income statement: continuing operations, discontinued operations, extraordinary items, and net income. Calculating Earnings per share

Chapter 1. What Is Strategy and the Strategic Management Process?

Chapter 1. What Is Strategy and the Strategic Management Process?

	The Earnings per share formula does not include preferred dividends for categories outside of continued operations and net income.
Gross profit	In accounting, gross profit is the difference between revenue and the cost of making a product or providing a service, before deducting overhead, payroll, taxation, and interest payments. Note that this is different from operating profit (earnings before interest and taxes).
	Net sales are calculated:
	Net sales = Gross sales - Sales of returns and allowances.
	Gross profit is found by deducting the cost of goods sold:
	Gross profit = Net sales - Cost of goods sold.
	Gross profit should not be confused with net income:
	Net income = Gross profit - Total operating expenses - taxes - interest.
	Cost of goods sold is calculated differently for merchandising business than for a manufacturer.
Inventory	In the USA and Canada the term has developed from a list of goods and materials to the goods and materials themselves, especially those held available in stock by a business; and this has become the primary meaning of the term in North American English, equivalent to the term 'stock' in British English. In accounting, inventory or stock is considered an asset.
	Inventory management is primarily about specifying the size and placement of stocked goods.

Chapter 1. What Is Strategy and the Strategic Management Process?

Chapter 1. What Is Strategy and the Strategic Management Process?

Inventory turnover	In accounting, the Inventory turnover is a measure of the number of times inventory is sold or used in a time period such as a year. The equation for inventory turnover equals the cost of goods sold divided by the average inventory. Inventory turnover is also known as inventory turns, stockturn, stock turns, turns, and stock turnover.
Price	In ordinary usage, price is the quantity of payment or compensation given by one party to another in return for goods or services.
	In all modern economies, the overwhelming majority of prices are quoted in (and the transactions involve) units of some form of currency. Although in theory, prices could be quoted as quantities of other goods or services this sort of barter exchange is rarely seen.
Returns	Returns, in economics and political economy, are the distributions or payments awarded to the various suppliers of the factors of production.
	Wages
	Wages are the return to labor--the return to an individual's involvement (mental or physical) in the creation or realization of goods or services. Wages are realized by an individual supplier of labor even if the supplier is the self.
Asset	An 'asset' in economic theory is an output good which can only be partially consumed (like a portable music player) or input as a factor of production (like a cement mixer) which can only be partially used up in production. The necessary quality for an asset is that value remain after the period of analysis so it can be used as a store of value. As such, financial instruments like corporate bonds and common stocks are assets because they store value for the next period.
Interest	Interest is a fee paid by a borrower of assets to the owner as a form of compensation for the use of the assets. It is most commonly the price paid for the use of borrowed money, or, money earned by deposited funds.

Chapter 1. What Is Strategy and the Strategic Management Process?

Chapter 1. What Is Strategy and the Strategic Management Process?

	When money is borrowed, interest is typically paid to the lender as a percentage of the principal, the amount owed.
Turnover	In a human resources context, turnover is the rate at which an employer gains and loses employees. Simple ways to describe it are 'how long employees tend to stay' or 'the rate of traffic through the revolving door.' Turnover is measured for individual companies and for their industry as a whole. If an employer is said to have a high turnover relative to its competitors, it means that employees of that company have a shorter average tenure than those of other companies in the same industry.
Average cost	In economics, average cost is equal to total cost divided by the number of goods produced (the output quantity, Q). It is also equal to the sum of average variable costs (total variable costs divided by Q) plus average fixed costs (total fixed costs divided by Q). Average costs may be dependent on the time period considered (increasing production may be expensive or impossible in the short term, for example).
Capital asset	The term capital asset has three unrelated technical definitions, and is also used in a variety of non-technical ways. • In financial economics, it refers to any asset used to make money, as opposed to assets used for personal enjoyment or consumption. This is an important distinction because two people can disagree sharply about the value of personal assets, one person might think a sports car is more valuable than a pickup truck, another person might have the opposite taste.
Capital asset pricing model	In finance, the capital asset pricing model is used to determine a theoretically appropriate required rate of return of an asset, if that asset is to be added to an already well-diversified portfolio, given that asset's non-diversifiable risk. The model takes into account the asset's sensitivity to non-diversifiable risk (also known as systematic risk or market risk), often represented by the quantity beta (β) in the financial industry, as well as the expected return of the market and the expected return of a theoretical risk-free asset.

Chapter 1. What Is Strategy and the Strategic Management Process?

Chapter 1. What Is Strategy and the Strategic Management Process?

	The model was introduced by Jack Treynor (1961, 1962), William Sharpe (1964), John Lintner (1965a,b) and Jan Mossin (1966) independently, building on the earlier work of Harry Markowitz on diversification and modern portfolio theory.
Pricing	Pricing is the process of determining what a company will receive in exchange for its products. Pricing factors are manufacturing cost, market place, competition, market condition, and quality of product. Pricing is also a key variable in microeconomic price allocation theory.
Stakeholder	A corporate stakeholder is a party that can affect or be affected by the actions of the business as a whole. The stakeholder concept was first used in a 1963 internal memorandum at the Stanford Research institute. It defined stakeholders as 'those groups without whose support the organization would cease to exist.' The theory was later developed and championed by R. Edward Freeman in the 1980s.
Entrepreneurship	Entrepreneurship is the act of being an entrepreneur, which can be defined as 'one who undertakes innovations, finance and business acumen in an effort to transform innovations into economic goods'. This may result in new organizations or may be part of revitalizing mature organizations in response to a perceived opportunity. The most obvious form of entrepreneurship is that of starting new businesses (referred as Startup Company); however, in recent years, the term has been extended to include social and political forms of entrepreneurial activity. When entrepreneurship is describing activities within a firm or large organization it is referred to as intra-preneurship and may include corporate venturing, when large entities spin-off organizations.

Chapter 1. What Is Strategy and the Strategic Management Process?

Chapter 2. Evaluating a Firm's External Environment

Demographics	Demographics are the characteristics of a human population. These types of data are used widely in sociology, public policy, and marketing. Commonly used demographics include gender, race, age, income, disabilities, mobility (in terms of travel time to work or number of vehicles available), educational attainment, home ownership, employment status, and even location.
Event	In probability theory, an event is a set of outcomes (a subset of the sample space) to which a probability is assigned. Typically, when the sample space is finite, any subset of the sample space is an event. However, this approach does not work well in cases where the sample space is uncountably infinite, most notably when the outcome is a real number.
Business cycle	The term business cycle refers to economy-wide fluctuations in production or economic activity over several months or years. These fluctuations occur around a long-term growth trend, and typically involve shifts over time between periods of relatively rapid economic growth (an expansion or boom), and periods of relative stagnation or decline (a contraction or recession). Business cycles are usually measured by considering the growth rate of real gross domestic product.
Chief executive	Chief Executive is a term used for certain gubernatorial offices, expressing the nature of their job being analogous to a head of government. Commonly used to refer to Presidential powers given by the constitution. As Chief Executive the president can: implement policy, supervise executive branch of government, prepare executive budget for submission to congress, and appoint and remove executive officials

Chapter 2. Evaluating a Firm's External Environment

Chapter 2. Evaluating a Firm's External Environment

	While in most cases there is another specific style, such as (lieutenant-)governor(-general), there are a few offices formally styled Chief Executive: • in the People's Republic of China, in two special administrative regions that were under foreign colonial rule until their recent transfer of sovereignty, where the chief executive are heads of the regions and heads of government: • in Mauritius, on Rodrigues island, since 12 October 2002 autonomy was granted: • New Zealand Antarctic Territory: while not a government, the Ross Dependency is a Crown entity managed by a Board of Directors and the Chair acts as the Chief Executive.
Chief executive officer	A chief executive officer, managing director, or chief executive is the highest-ranking corporate officer (executive) or administrator in charge of total management of an organization. An individual appointed as a Chief executive officer of a corporation, company, organization, or agency reports to the board of directors. Many Chief executive officers have the title 'president and Chief executive officer'.
Executive officer	An executive officer is generally a person responsible for running an organization, although the exact nature of the role varies depending on the organization. Administrative law While there is no clear line between executive or principal and inferior officers, principal officers are high-level officials in the executive branch of U.S. government such as department heads of independent agencies. In Humphrey's Executor v. United States, 295 U.S. 602 (1935), the Court distinguished between executive officers and quasi-legislative or quasi-judicial officers by stating that the former serve at the pleasure of the President and may be removed at his discretion.

Chapter 2. Evaluating a Firm`s External Environment

Chapter 2. Evaluating a Firm's External Environment

Competitive advantage	Competitive advantage is defined as the strategic advantage one business entity has over its rival entities within its competitive industry. Achieving competitive advantage strengthens and positions a business better within the business environment. Resource-based view perspective Competitive advantage is a theory that seeks to address some of the criticisms of comparative advantage.
Vendor	A vendor, is a supply chain management term meaning anyone who provides goods or services to a company. A vendor often manufactures inventoriable items, and sells those items to a customer. History The term vendor originally represented property vendors.
Perfect competition	In economic theory, perfect competition describes markets such that no participants are large enough to have the market power to set the price of a homogeneous product. Because the conditions for perfect competition are strict, there are few if any perfectly competitive markets. Still, buyers and sellers in some auction-type markets, say for commodities or some financial assets, may approximate the concept.
Barriers to entry	In theories of competition in economics, barriers to entry are obstacles that make it difficult to enter a given market. The term can refer to hindrances a firm faces in trying to enter a market or industry - such as government regulation, or a large, established firm taking advantage of economies of scale - or those an individual faces in trying to gain entrance to a profession - such as education or licensing requirements. Because barriers to entry protect incumbent firms and restrict competition in a market, they can contribute to distortionary prices.

Chapter 2. Evaluating a Firm's External Environment

Chapter 2. Evaluating a Firm's External Environment

Cost leadership	Cost leadership is a concept developed by Michael Porter, used in business strategy. It describes a way to establish the competitive advantage. Cost leadership, in basic words, means the lowest cost of operation in the industry.
Economies of scale	Economies of scale, in microeconomics, refers to the cost advantages that a business obtains due to expansion. There are factors that cause a producer's average cost per unit to fall as the scale of output is increased. 'Economies of scale' is a long run concept and refers to reductions in unit cost as the size of a facility and the usage levels of other inputs increase.
Leadership	Leadership has been described as the 'process of social influence in which one person can enlist the aid and support of others in the accomplishment of a common task'. Definitions more inclusive of followers have also emerged. Alan Keith of Genentech states that, 'Leadership is ultimately about creating a way for people to contribute to making something extraordinary happen.' According to Ken 'SKC' Ogbonnia, 'effective leadership is the ability to successfully integrate and maximize available resources within the internal and external environment for the attainment of organizational or societal goals.' The following sections discuss several important aspects of leadership including a description of what leadership is and a description of several popular theories and styles of leadership.
Product	The noun product is defined as a 'thing produced by labor or effort' or the 'result of an act or a process', and stems from the verb produce, from the Latin produce(re) '(to) lead or bring forth'. Since 1575, the word 'product' has referred to anything produced. Since 1695, the word has referred to 'thing or things produced'.
Product differentiation	In economics and marketing, product differentiation is the process of distinguishing a product or offering from others, to make it more attractive to a particular target market. This involves differentiating it from competitors' products as well as a firm's own product offerings. The concept was proposed by Edward Chamberlin in his 1933 Theory of Monopolistic Competition.

Chapter 2. Evaluating a Firm's External Environment

Chapter 2. Evaluating a Firm's External Environment

Access	Access is a catalytic process that enables interactions, contacts and exchanges among people, businesses and nations. An analytical framework to define the drivers and benefits of Access and to quantify the impact of Access on economic growth and personal well-being was created in 2006 by the Center for Science, Technology, and Economic Development at SRI International (formerly known as the Stanford Research Institute) in its study, 'The Power of Access' (also titled, 'How Greater Access Is Changing The World: A Landmark Study on the Relevance of Access to People, Businesses and Nations'). As outlined in the study, the Access framework consists of the Access Model, which expresses the function of Access as an econometric equation; the 'Access Cycle'; and the 'Access Index,' which ranks 75 nations based on their performance in 22 metrics, including transportation infrastructure; telecommunications networks; trade policy; and news, media and information services.
Raw material	A raw material is acted upon or used by human labor or industry, for use as the basis to create some product or structure. Often the term is used to denote material that came from nature and is in an unprocessed or minimally processed state. Latex, iron ore, logs, and crude oil, would be examples.
Policy	A policy is typically described as a principle or rule to guide decisions and achieve rational outcome(s). The term is not normally used to denote what is actually done, this is normally referred to as either procedure or protocol. Whereas a policy will contain the 'what' and the 'why', procedures or protocols contain the 'what', the 'how', the 'where', and the 'when'.
Embedded system	An embedded system is a computer system designed to do one or a few dedicated and/or specific functions often with real-time computing constraints. It is embedded as part of a complete device often including hardware and mechanical parts. By contrast, a general-purpose computer, such as a personal computer (PC), is designed to be flexible and to meet a wide range of end-user needs.
Arbitration	Arbitration, a form of alternative dispute resolution (ADR), is a legal technique for the resolution of disputes outside the courts, where the parties to a dispute refer it to one or more persons (the 'arbitrators', 'arbiters' or 'arbitral tribunal'), by whose decision (the 'award') they agree to be bound. It is a settlement technique in which a third party reviews the case and imposes a decision that is legally binding for both sides. Other forms of ADR include mediation (a form of settlement negotiation facilitated by a neutral third party) and non-binding resolution by experts.
Delivery	Delivery is the process of transporting goods. Most goods are delivered through a transportation network. Cargo (physical goods) are primarily delivered via roads and railroads on land, shipping lanes on the sea and airline networks in the air.

Chapter 2. Evaluating a Firm's External Environment

Chapter 2. Evaluating a Firm's External Environment

Financial planning	Financial planning is the task of determining how a business will afford to achieve its strategic goals and objectives. Usually, a company creates a Financial Plan immediately after the vision and objectives have been set. The Financial Plan describes each of the activities, resources, equipment and materials that are needed to achieve these objectives, as well as the timeframes involved.
Mediation	Mediation, as used in law, is a form of alternative dispute resolution (ADR), is a way of resolving disputes between two or more parties. A third party, the mediator, assists the parties to negotiate their own settlement (facilitative mediation). In some cases, mediators may express a view on what might be a fair or reasonable settlement, generally where all the parties agree that the mediator may do so (evaluative mediation).
Planner	Planner is the GNOME project management tool. It's a GTK+ application written in C and licensed under the GPLv2 or any later version. History Planner was originally created by Richard Hult and Mikael Hallendal at Imendio and now managed by GNOME. Features Planner can store its data in either XML files or in a PostgreSQL database.
Shopping	Shopping is the examining of goods or services from retailers with the intent to purchase at that time. Shopping is an activity of selection and/or purchase. In some contexts it is considered a leisure activity as well as an economic one.
Vertical integration	In microeconomics and management, the term vertical integration describes a style of management control. Vertically integrated companies in a supply chain are united through a common owner. Usually each member of the supply chain produces a different product or (market-specific) service, and the products combine to satisfy a common need.

Chapter 2. Evaluating a Firm's External Environment

Chapter 2. Evaluating a Firm's External Environment

Complementors	Complementors is a term used to describe businesses that directly sell a product (or products) or service (or services) that complement the product or service of another company by adding value to mutual customers; for example, Intel and Microsoft (Pentium processors and Windows), or Microsoft ' McAfee (Microsoft Windows ' McAfee anti-virus). Complementors are sometimes called 'The Sixth Force' (from Porter's Five Forces model), a term which was coined by Adam Brandenburger. Before its use in business, the word was used to describe a color that is complementory to another color.
First-mover advantage	First-mover advantage is the advantage gained by the initial ('first-moving') significant occupant of a market segment. This advantage may stem from the fact that the first entrant can gain control of resources that followers may not be able to match. Sometimes the first mover is not able to capitalize on its advantage, leaving the opportunity for another firm to gain second-mover advantage.
Asset	An 'asset' in economic theory is an output good which can only be partially consumed (like a portable music player) or input as a factor of production (like a cement mixer) which can only be partially used up in production. The necessary quality for an asset is that value remain after the period of analysis so it can be used as a store of value. As such, financial instruments like corporate bonds and common stocks are assets because they store value for the next period.
Refining	Refining is the process of purification of a (1) substance or a (2) form. The term is usually used of a natural resource that is almost in a usable form, but which is more useful in its pure form. For instance, most types of natural petroleum will burn straight from the ground, but it will burn poorly and quickly clog an engine with residues and by-products.
General Architecture for Text Engineering	General Architecture for Text Engineering is a Java suite of tools originally developed at the University of Sheffield beginning in 1995 and now used worldwide by a wide community of scientists, companies, teachers and students for all sorts of natural language processing tasks, including information extraction in many languages.

Chapter 2. Evaluating a Firm's External Environment

Chapter 2. Evaluating a Firm's External Environment

GATE includes:

- an IDE, GATE Developer: an integrated development environment for natural language processing components bundled with a very widely used information extraction system and a comprehensive set of other plugins
- a web app, GATE Teamware: a collaborative annotation environment for factory-style semantic annotation projects built around a workflow engine and a heavily-optimised backend service infrastructure
- a framework, GATE Embedded: an object library optimised for inclusion in diverse applications giving access to all the services used by GATE Developer and more
- an architecture: a high-level organisational picture of language processing software composition
- a process for the creation of robust and maintainable services.

Under development:

- a wiki/CMS
- a cloud computing solution for hosted large-scale text processing, GATE Cloud

GATE aims to remove the necessity for solving common engineering problems before doing useful research, or re-engineering before deploying research results into applications.

Innovation	In time series analysis (or forecasting) -- as conducted in statistics, signal processing, and many other fields -- the innovation is the difference between the observed value of a variable at time t and the optimal forecast of that value based on information available prior to time t. If the forecasting method is working correctly successive innovations are uncorrelated with each other, i.e., constitute a white noise time series. Thus it can be said that the innovation time series is obtained from the measurement time series by a process of 'whitening', or removing the predictable component.
Market	A market is any one of a variety of systems, institutions, procedures, social relations and infrastructures whereby parties engage in exchange. While parties may exchange goods and services by barter, most markets rely on buyers offer their goods or services (including labor) in exchange for money (legal tender such as fiat money) from buyers.

Chapter 2. Evaluating a Firm's External Environment

Chapter 2. Evaluating a Firm's External Environment

	For a market to be competitive, there must be more than a single buyer or seller.
Divestment	In finance and economics, divestment is the reduction of some kind of asset for either financial or ethical objectives or sale of an existing business by a firm. A divestment is the opposite of an investment. Motives Firms may have several motives for divestitures.
Diversification	In finance, diversification means reducing risk by investing in a variety of assets. If the asset values do not move up and down in perfect synchrony, a diversified portfolio will have less risk than the weighted average risk of its constituent assets, and often less risk than the least risky of its constituents.. Therefore, any risk-averse investor will diversify to at least some extent, with more risk-averse investors diversifying more completely than less risk-averse investors.
Trade barrier	Trade barriers are a general term that describes any government policy or regulation that restricts international trade. The barriers can take many forms, including the following terms that include many restrictions in international trade within multiple countries that import and export any items of trade: - Tariffs - Non-tariff barriers to trade - Import licenses - Export licenses - Import quotas - Subsidies - Voluntary Export Restraints - Local content requirements - Embargo

Chapter 2. Evaluating a Firm`s External Environment

Chapter 2. Evaluating a Firm`s External Environment

Most trade barriers work on the same principle: the imposition of some sort of cost on trade that raises the price of the traded products. If two or more nations repeatedly use trade barriers against each other, then a trade war results.

Chapter 2. Evaluating a Firm's External Environment

Chapter 3. Evaluating a Firm's Internal Capabilities

Resource-based view	The resource-based view is a business management tool used to determine the strategic resources available to a company. The fundamental principle of the Resource based view is that the basis for a competitive advantage of a firm lies primarily in the application of the bundle of valuable resources at the firm's disposal (Wernerfelt, 1984, p172; Rumelt, 1984, p557-558). To transform a short-run competitive advantage into a sustained competitive advantage requires that these resources are heterogeneous in nature and not perfectly mobile (:p105-106; Peteraf, 1993, p180).
Resource	In project management terminology, resources are required to carry out the project tasks. They can be people, equipment, facilities, funding, or anything else capable of definition (usually other than labour) required for the completion of a project activity. The lack of a resource will therefore be a constraint on the completion of the project activity.
General Architecture for Text Engineering	General Architecture for Text Engineering is a Java suite of tools originally developed at the University of Sheffield beginning in 1995 and now used worldwide by a wide community of scientists, companies, teachers and students for all sorts of natural language processing tasks, including information extraction in many languages. GATE includes: - an IDE, GATE Developer: an integrated development environment for natural language processing components bundled with a very widely used information extraction system and a comprehensive set of other plugins - a web app, GATE Teamware: a collaborative annotation environment for factory-style semantic annotation projects built around a workflow engine and a heavily-optimised backend service infrastructure - a framework, GATE Embedded: an object library optimised for inclusion in diverse applications giving access to all the services used by GATE Developer and more - an architecture: a high-level organisational picture of language processing software composition - a process for the creation of robust and maintainable services. Under development: - a wiki/CMS - a cloud computing solution for hosted large-scale text processing, GATE Cloud

Chapter 3. Evaluating a Firm's Internal Capabilities

Chapter 3. Evaluating a Firm's Internal Capabilities

	GATE aims to remove the necessity for solving common engineering problems before doing useful research, or re-engineering before deploying research results into applications.
Human resources	Human resources is a term used to describe the individuals who make up the workforce of an organization, although it is also applied in labor economics to, for example, business sectors or even whole nations. Human resources is also the name of the function within an organization charged with the overall responsibility for implementing strategies and policies relating to the management of individuals (i.e. the human resources). This function title is often abbreviated to the initials .
Question	A question may be either a linguistic expression used to make a request for information, or else the request itself made by such an expression. This information is provided with an answer. Questions are normally put forward or asked using interrogative sentences.
Market	A market is any one of a variety of systems, institutions, procedures, social relations and infrastructures whereby parties engage in exchange. While parties may exchange goods and services by barter, most markets rely on buyers offer their goods or services (including labor) in exchange for money (legal tender such as fiat money) from buyers. For a market to be competitive, there must be more than a single buyer or seller.
Value chain	The value chain, is a concept from business management that was first described and popularized by Michael Porter in his 1985 best-seller, Competitive Advantage: Creating and Sustaining Superior Performance. Firm Level

Chapter 3. Evaluating a Firm's Internal Capabilities

Chapter 3. Evaluating a Firm's Internal Capabilities

	A value chain is a chain of activities for a firm operating in a specific industry. The business unit is the appropriate level for construction of a value chain, not the divisional level or corporate level.
Profit maximization	In economics, profit maximization is the (short run) process by which a firm determines the price and output level that returns the greatest profit. There are several approaches to this problem. The total revenue-total cost method relies on the fact that profit equals revenue minus cost, and the marginal revenue-marginal cost method is based on the fact that total profit in a perfectly competitive market reaches its maximum point where marginal revenue equals marginal cost.
Competitive advantage	Competitive advantage is defined as the strategic advantage one business entity has over its rival entities within its competitive industry. Achieving competitive advantage strengthens and positions a business better within the business environment. Resource-based view perspective Competitive advantage is a theory that seeks to address some of the criticisms of comparative advantage.
Path dependence	Path dependence explains how the set of decisions one faces for any given circumstance is limited by the decisions one has made in the past, even though past circumstances may no longer be relevant. In economics and the social sciences path dependence can refer to either outcomes at a single moment in time or to long run equilibria of a process (Page 2006). In common usage, the phrase implies either: - (A) that 'history matters' - a broad concept, or - (B) that predictable amplifications of small differences are a disproportionate cause of later circumstances.

Chapter 3. Evaluating a Firm's Internal Capabilities

Chapter 3. Evaluating a Firm's Internal Capabilities

Resource management	In organizational studies, resource management is the efficient and effective deployment for an organization's resources when they are needed. Such resources may include financial resources, inventory, human skills, production resources, or information technology (IT). In the realm of project management, processes, techniques and philosophies as to the best approach for allocating resources have been developed.
Management control system	A management control systems is a system which gathers and uses information to evaluate the performance of different organizational resources like human, physical, financial and also the organization as a whole considering the organizational strategies. Finally, Management control system influences the behavior of organizational resources to implement organizational strategies. Management control system might be formal or informal.
Organizational chart	An organizational chart (often called organization chart, org chart, organigram(me), or organogram(me)) is a diagram that shows the structure of an organization and the relationships and relative ranks of its parts and positions/jobs. The term is also used for similar diagrams, for example ones showing the different elements of a field of knowledge or a group of languages. The French Encyclopédie had one of the first organizational charts of knowledge in general.
Competence	Competence is the ability of an individual to perform a job properly. The term has been popular since its use by Richard Boyatzis. Its use varies widely, which leads to considerable misunderstanding.
Tacit collusion	Tacit collusion occurs when cartels are illegal or overt collusion is absent. Put another way, two firms agree to play a certain strategy without explicitly saying so. Oligopolists usually try not to engage in price cutting, excessive advertising or other forms of competition.
Collusion	Collusion is an agreement between two or more persons, sometimes illegal and therefore secretive, to limit open competition by deceiving, misleading, or defrauding others of their legal rights, or to obtain an objective forbidden by law typically by defrauding or gaining an unfair advantage. It is an agreement among firms to divide the market, set prices, or limit production. It can involve 'wage fixing, kickbacks, or misrepresenting the independence of the relationship between the colluding parties'.
Diversification	In finance, diversification means reducing risk by investing in a variety of assets. If the asset values do not move up and down in perfect synchrony, a diversified portfolio will have less risk than the weighted average risk of its constituent assets, and often less risk than the least risky of its constituents.. Therefore, any risk-averse investor will diversify to at least some extent, with more risk-averse investors diversifying more completely than less risk-averse investors.

Chapter 3. Evaluating a Firm`s Internal Capabilities

Chapter 4. Cost Leadership

Cost leadership	Cost leadership is a concept developed by Michael Porter, used in business strategy. It describes a way to establish the competitive advantage. Cost leadership, in basic words, means the lowest cost of operation in the industry.
Leadership	Leadership has been described as the 'process of social influence in which one person can enlist the aid and support of others in the accomplishment of a common task'. Definitions more inclusive of followers have also emerged. Alan Keith of Genentech states that, 'Leadership is ultimately about creating a way for people to contribute to making something extraordinary happen.' According to Ken 'SKC' Ogbonnia, 'effective leadership is the ability to successfully integrate and maximize available resources within the internal and external environment for the attainment of organizational or societal goals.'
	The following sections discuss several important aspects of leadership including a description of what leadership is and a description of several popular theories and styles of leadership.
Economies of scale	Economies of scale, in microeconomics, refers to the cost advantages that a business obtains due to expansion. There are factors that cause a producer's average cost per unit to fall as the scale of output is increased. 'Economies of scale' is a long run concept and refers to reductions in unit cost as the size of a facility and the usage levels of other inputs increase.
Overhead	In business, overhead, overhead cost or overhead expense refers to an ongoing expense of operating a business (also known as Operating Expenses - rent, gas/electricity, wages etc).. The term overhead is usually used to group expenses that are necessary to the continued functioning of the business, but cannot be immediately associated with the products/services being offered (e.g. do not directly generate profits). Closely related accounting concepts are fixed costs versus variable costs and indirect costs versus direct costs.
Competitive advantage	Competitive advantage is defined as the strategic advantage one business entity has over its rival entities within its competitive industry. Achieving competitive advantage strengthens and positions a business better within the business environment.
	Resource-based view perspective

Chapter 4. Cost Leadership

Chapter 4. Cost Leadership

Competitive advantage is a theory that seeks to address some of the criticisms of comparative advantage.

Access

Access is a catalytic process that enables interactions, contacts and exchanges among people, businesses and nations. An analytical framework to define the drivers and benefits of Access and to quantify the impact of Access on economic growth and personal well-being was created in 2006 by the Center for Science, Technology, and Economic Development at SRI International (formerly known as the Stanford Research Institute) in its study, 'The Power of Access' (also titled, 'How Greater Access Is Changing The World: A Landmark Study on the Relevance of Access to People, Businesses and Nations'). As outlined in the study, the Access framework consists of the Access Model, which expresses the function of Access as an econometric equation; the 'Access Cycle'; and the 'Access Index,' which ranks 75 nations based on their performance in 22 metrics, including transportation infrastructure; telecommunications networks; trade policy; and news, media and information services.

Raw material

A raw material is acted upon or used by human labor or industry, for use as the basis to create some product or structure. Often the term is used to denote material that came from nature and is in an unprocessed or minimally processed state. Latex, iron ore, logs, and crude oil, would be examples.

Policy

A policy is typically described as a principle or rule to guide decisions and achieve rational outcome(s). The term is not normally used to denote what is actually done, this is normally referred to as either procedure or protocol. Whereas a policy will contain the 'what' and the 'why', procedures or protocols contain the 'what', the 'how', the 'where', and the 'when'.

Vendor

A vendor, is a supply chain management term meaning anyone who provides goods or services to a company. A vendor often manufactures inventoriable items, and sells those items to a customer.

History

The term vendor originally represented property vendors.

Chapter 4. Cost Leadership

Chapter 4. Cost Leadership

Vertical integration	In microeconomics and management, the term vertical integration describes a style of management control. Vertically integrated companies in a supply chain are united through a common owner. Usually each member of the supply chain produces a different product or (market-specific) service, and the products combine to satisfy a common need.
Escalation	Escalation is the phenomenon of something getting more intense step by step, for example a quarrel, or, notably, a war between states possessing weapons of mass destruction. Compare to escalator, a device that lifts something to a higher level.
Escalation of commitment	Escalation of commitment was first described by Barry M. Staw in his 1976 paper, 'Knee deep in the big muddy: A study of escalating commitment to a chosen course of action'. More recently the term sunk cost fallacy has been used to describe the phenomenon where people justify increased investment in a decision, based on the cumulative prior investment, despite new evidence suggesting that the cost, starting today, of continuing the decision outweighs the expected benefit. Such investment may include money, time, or -- in the case of military strategy -- human lives.
Organizational structure	An organizational structure consists of activities such as task allocation, coordination and supervision, which are directed towards the achievement of organizational aims. It can also be considered as the viewing glass or perspective through which individuals see their organization and its environment. Many organizations have hierarchical structures, but not all.
Chief executive	Chief Executive is a term used for certain gubernatorial offices, expressing the nature of their job being analogous to a head of government. Commonly used to refer to Presidential powers given by the constitution. As Chief Executive the president can: implement policy, supervise executive branch of government, prepare executive budget for submission to congress, and appoint and remove executive officials

Chapter 4. Cost Leadership

Chapter 4. Cost Leadership

While in most cases there is another specific style, such as (lieutenant-)governor(-general), there are a few offices formally styled Chief Executive:

- in the People's Republic of China, in two special administrative regions that were under foreign colonial rule until their recent transfer of sovereignty, where the chief executive are heads of the regions and heads of government:

- in Mauritius, on Rodrigues island, since 12 October 2002 autonomy was granted:

- New Zealand Antarctic Territory: while not a government, the Ross Dependency is a Crown entity managed by a Board of Directors and the Chair acts as the Chief Executive.

Chief executive officer

A chief executive officer, managing director, or chief executive is the highest-ranking corporate officer (executive) or administrator in charge of total management of an organization. An individual appointed as a Chief executive officer of a corporation, company, organization, or agency reports to the board of directors.

Many Chief executive officers have the title 'president and Chief executive officer'.

Executive officer

An executive officer is generally a person responsible for running an organization, although the exact nature of the role varies depending on the organization.

Administrative law

While there is no clear line between executive or principal and inferior officers, principal officers are high-level officials in the executive branch of U.S. government such as department heads of independent agencies. In Humphrey's Executor v. United States, 295 U.S. 602 (1935), the Court distinguished between executive officers and quasi-legislative or quasi-judicial officers by stating that the former serve at the pleasure of the President and may be removed at his discretion.

Chapter 4. Cost Leadership

Chapter 4. Cost Leadership

Diversification	In finance, diversification means reducing risk by investing in a variety of assets. If the asset values do not move up and down in perfect synchrony, a diversified portfolio will have less risk than the weighted average risk of its constituent assets, and often less risk than the least risky of its constituents.. Therefore, any risk-averse investor will diversify to at least some extent, with more risk-averse investors diversifying more completely than less risk-averse investors.
Management control system	A management control systems is a system which gathers and uses information to evaluate the performance of different organizational resources like human, physical, financial and also the organization as a whole considering the organizational strategies. Finally, Management control system influences the behavior of organizational resources to implement organizational strategies. Management control system might be formal or informal.

Chapter 4. Cost Leadership

Chapter 5. Product Differentiation

Product	The noun product is defined as a 'thing produced by labor or effort' or the 'result of an act or a process', and stems from the verb produce, from the Latin produce(re) '(to) lead or bring forth'. Since 1575, the word 'product' has referred to anything produced. Since 1695, the word has referred to 'thing or things produced'.
Product differentiation	In economics and marketing, product differentiation is the process of distinguishing a product or offering from others, to make it more attractive to a particular target market. This involves differentiating it from competitors' products as well as a firm's own product offerings. The concept was proposed by Edward Chamberlin in his 1933 Theory of Monopolistic Competition.
Market	A market is any one of a variety of systems, institutions, procedures, social relations and infrastructures whereby parties engage in exchange. While parties may exchange goods and services by barter, most markets rely on buyers offer their goods or services (including labor) in exchange for money (legal tender such as fiat money) from buyers. For a market to be competitive, there must be more than a single buyer or seller.
Linear regression	In statistics, linear regression is an approach to modeling the relationship between a scalar variable y and one or more variables denoted X. In linear regression, data are modeled using linear functions, and unknown model parameters are estimated from the data. Such models are called linear models. Most commonly, linear regression refers to a model in which the conditional mean of y given the value of X is an affine function of X. Less commonly, linear regression could refer to a model in which the median, or some other quantile of the conditional distribution of y given X is expressed as a linear function of X. Like all forms of regression analysis, linear regression focuses on the conditional probability distribution of y given X, rather than on the joint probability distribution of y and X, which is the domain of multivariate analysis.
Price	In ordinary usage, price is the quantity of payment or compensation given by one party to another in return for goods or services.

Chapter 5. Product Differentiation

Chapter 5. Product Differentiation

	In all modern economies, the overwhelming majority of prices are quoted in (and the transactions involve) units of some form of currency. Although in theory, prices could be quoted as quantities of other goods or services this sort of barter exchange is rarely seen.
Marketing	Marketing is the process of performing market research, selling products and/or services to customers and promoting them via advertising to further enhance sales. It generates the strategy that underlies sales techniques, business communication, and business developments. It is an integrated process through which companies build strong customer relationships and create value for their customers and for themselves.
Competence	Competence is the ability of an individual to perform a job properly. The term has been popular since its use by Richard Boyatzis. Its use varies widely, which leads to considerable misunderstanding.
Distribution	Product distribution is one of the four elements of the marketing mix. An organization or set of organizations (go-betweens) involved in the process of making a product or service available for use or consumption by a consumer or business user. The other three parts of the marketing mix are product, pricing, and promotion.
Shopping	Shopping is the examining of goods or services from retailers with the intent to purchase at that time. Shopping is an activity of selection and/or purchase. In some contexts it is considered a leisure activity as well as an economic one.
Shopping mall	A shopping mall, shopping centre, shopping precinct or simply mall is one or more buildings forming a complex of shops representing merchandisers, with interconnecting walkways enabling visitors to easily walk from unit to unit, along with a parking area - a modern, indoor version of the traditional marketplace.

Chapter 5. Product Differentiation

Chapter 5. Product Differentiation

	Modern 'car-friendly' strip malls developed from the 1920s, and shopping malls corresponded with the rise of suburban living in many parts of the Western World, especially the United States, after World War II. From early on, the design tended to be inward-facing, with malls following theories of how customers could best be enticed in a controlled environment. Similar, the concept of a mall having one or more 'anchor' or 'big box' stores was pioneered early, with individual stores or smaller-scale chain stores intended to benefit from the shoppers attracted by the big stores.
Cost leadership	Cost leadership is a concept developed by Michael Porter, used in business strategy. It describes a way to establish the competitive advantage. Cost leadership, in basic words, means the lowest cost of operation in the industry.
Leadership	Leadership has been described as the 'process of social influence in which one person can enlist the aid and support of others in the accomplishment of a common task'. Definitions more inclusive of followers have also emerged. Alan Keith of Genentech states that, 'Leadership is ultimately about creating a way for people to contribute to making something extraordinary happen.' According to Ken 'SKC' Ogbonnia, 'effective leadership is the ability to successfully integrate and maximize available resources within the internal and external environment for the attainment of organizational or societal goals.' The following sections discuss several important aspects of leadership including a description of what leadership is and a description of several popular theories and styles of leadership.
Vendor	A vendor, is a supply chain management term meaning anyone who provides goods or services to a company. A vendor often manufactures inventoriable items, and sells those items to a customer. History The term vendor originally represented property vendors.

Chapter 5. Product Differentiation

Chapter 5. Product Differentiation

Competitive advantage	Competitive advantage is defined as the strategic advantage one business entity has over its rival entities within its competitive industry. Achieving competitive advantage strengthens and positions a business better within the business environment. Resource-based view perspective Competitive advantage is a theory that seeks to address some of the criticisms of comparative advantage.
Organizational structure	An organizational structure consists of activities such as task allocation, coordination and supervision, which are directed towards the achievement of organizational aims. It can also be considered as the viewing glass or perspective through which individuals see their organization and its environment. Many organizations have hierarchical structures, but not all.
Cross-functional team	A cross-functional team is a group of people with different functional expertise working toward a common goal. It may include people from finance, marketing, operations, and human resources departments. Typically, it includes employees from all levels of an organization.
TEAM	TEAM, formerly known as Team of Destiny, is a leadership development company founded by Orrin Woodward and Chris Brady in 1999 in Michigan. TEAM is an acronym that stands for TEAM. Woodward and Brady are former IBOs (Independent Business Owners, a.k.a. distributors) of the multi-level marketing company Quixtar, as well as members of the board of directors of Quixtar's IBOAI (IBO Association International, representing Quixtar IBOs).

Chapter 5. Product Differentiation

Chapter 5. Product Differentiation

Incentive	In economics and sociology, an incentive is any factor (financial or non-financial) that enables or motivates a particular course of action, or counts as a reason for preferring one choice to the alternatives. It is an expectation that encourages people to behave in a certain way. Since human beings are purposeful creatures, the study of incentive structures is central to the study of all economic activity (both in terms of individual decision-making and in terms of co-operation and competition within a larger institutional structure).
Innovation	In time series analysis (or forecasting) -- as conducted in statistics, signal processing, and many other fields -- the innovation is the difference between the observed value of a variable at time t and the optimal forecast of that value based on information available prior to time t. If the forecasting method is working correctly successive innovations are uncorrelated with each other, i.e., constitute a white noise time series. Thus it can be said that the innovation time series is obtained from the measurement time series by a process of 'whitening', or removing the predictable component.
Policy	A policy is typically described as a principle or rule to guide decisions and achieve rational outcome(s). The term is not normally used to denote what is actually done, this is normally referred to as either procedure or protocol. Whereas a policy will contain the 'what' and the 'why', procedures or protocols contain the 'what', the 'how', the 'where', and the 'when'.
Market share	Market share, in strategic management and marketing is, according to Carlton O'Neal, the percentage or proportion of the total available market or market segment that is being serviced by a company. It can be expressed as a company's sales revenue (from that market) divided by the total sales revenue available in that market. It can also be expressed as a company's unit sales volume (in a market) divided by the total volume of units sold in that market.
Diversification	In finance, diversification means reducing risk by investing in a variety of assets. If the asset values do not move up and down in perfect synchrony, a diversified portfolio will have less risk than the weighted average risk of its constituent assets, and often less risk than the least risky of its constituents.. Therefore, any risk-averse investor will diversify to at least some extent, with more risk-averse investors diversifying more completely than less risk-averse investors.
International marketing	International marketing or global marketing refers to marketing carried out by companies overseas or across national borderlines. This strategy uses an extension of the techniques used in the home country of a firm. It refers to the firm-level marketing practices across the border including market identification and targeting, entry mode selection, marketing mix, and strategic decisions to compete in international markets.
Standardization	Standardization is the process of developing and implementing technical standards.

Chapter 5. Product Differentiation

Chapter 5. Product Differentiation

The goals of standardization can be to help with independence of single suppliers (commoditization), compatibility, interoperability, safety, repeatability, or quality.

In social sciences, including economics, the idea of standardization is close to the solution for a coordination problem, a situation in which all parties can realize mutual gains, but only by making mutually consistent decisions.

Chapter 5. Product Differentiation

Chapter 6. Vertical Integration

Vertical integration	In microeconomics and management, the term vertical integration describes a style of management control. Vertically integrated companies in a supply chain are united through a common owner. Usually each member of the supply chain produces a different product or (market-specific) service, and the products combine to satisfy a common need.
Value chain	The value chain, is a concept from business management that was first described and popularized by Michael Porter in his 1985 best-seller, Competitive Advantage: Creating and Sustaining Superior Performance.
	Firm Level
	A value chain is a chain of activities for a firm operating in a specific industry. The business unit is the appropriate level for construction of a value chain, not the divisional level or corporate level.
Diversification	In finance, diversification means reducing risk by investing in a variety of assets. If the asset values do not move up and down in perfect synchrony, a diversified portfolio will have less risk than the weighted average risk of its constituent assets, and often less risk than the least risky of its constituents.. Therefore, any risk-averse investor will diversify to at least some extent, with more risk-averse investors diversifying more completely than less risk-averse investors.
Investment	Investment is putting money into something with the expectation of profit. More specifically, investment is the commitment of money or capital to the purchase of financial instruments or other assets so as to gain profitable returns in the form of interest, dividends, or appreciation of the value of the instrument (capital gains). It is related to saving or deferring consumption. Investment is involved in many areas of the economy, such as business management and finance whether for households, firms, or governments. An investment involves the choice by an individual or an organization, such as a pension fund, after some analysis or thought, to place or lend money in a vehicle, instrument or asset, such as property, commodity, stock, bond, financial derivatives (e.g. futures or options), or the foreign asset denominated in foreign currency, that has certain level of risk and provides the possibility of generating returns over a period of time.

Chapter 6. Vertical Integration

Chapter 6. Vertical Integration

Competitive advantage	Competitive advantage is defined as the strategic advantage one business entity has over its rival entities within its competitive industry. Achieving competitive advantage strengthens and positions a business better within the business environment. Resource-based view perspective Competitive advantage is a theory that seeks to address some of the criticisms of comparative advantage.
Outsourcing	Outsourcing or sub-servicing often refers to the process of contracting to a third-party. Overview A precise definition of outsourcing has yet to be agreed upon. Thus, the term is used inconsistently.
Organizational structure	An organizational structure consists of activities such as task allocation, coordination and supervision, which are directed towards the achievement of organizational aims. It can also be considered as the viewing glass or perspective through which individuals see their organization and its environment. Many organizations have hierarchical structures, but not all.
Chief executive	Chief Executive is a term used for certain gubernatorial offices, expressing the nature of their job being analogous to a head of government. Commonly used to refer to Presidential powers given by the constitution. As Chief Executive the president can: implement policy, supervise executive branch of government, prepare executive budget for submission to congress, and appoint and remove executive officials

Chapter 6. Vertical Integration

Chapter 6. Vertical Integration

While in most cases there is another specific style, such as (lieutenant-)governor(-general), there are a few offices formally styled Chief Executive:

- in the People's Republic of China, in two special administrative regions that were under foreign colonial rule until their recent transfer of sovereignty, where the chief executive are heads of the regions and heads of government:

- in Mauritius, on Rodrigues island, since 12 October 2002 autonomy was granted:

- New Zealand Antarctic Territory: while not a government, the Ross Dependency is a Crown entity managed by a Board of Directors and the Chair acts as the Chief Executive.

Executive officer	An executive officer is generally a person responsible for running an organization, although the exact nature of the role varies depending on the organization. Administrative law While there is no clear line between executive or principal and inferior officers, principal officers are high-level officials in the executive branch of U.S. government such as department heads of independent agencies. In Humphrey's Executor v. United States, 295 U.S. 602 (1935), the Court distinguished between executive officers and quasi-legislative or quasi-judicial officers by stating that the former serve at the pleasure of the President and may be removed at his discretion.
Process management	Process management is the ensemble of activities of planning and monitoring the performance of a process. The term usually refers to the management of business processes and manufacturing processes. Business process management and business process reengineering are interrelated, but not identical.
Chief executive officer	A chief executive officer, managing director, or chief executive is the highest-ranking corporate officer (executive) or administrator in charge of total management of an organization. An individual appointed as a Chief executive officer of a corporation, company, organization, or agency reports to the board of directors.

Chapter 6. Vertical Integration

Chapter 6. Vertical Integration

	Many Chief executive officers have the title 'president and Chief executive officer'.
Product	The noun product is defined as a 'thing produced by labor or effort' or the 'result of an act or a process', and stems from the verb produce, from the Latin produce(re) '(to) lead or bring forth'. Since 1575, the word 'product' has referred to anything produced. Since 1695, the word has referred to 'thing or things produced'.
Product differentiation	In economics and marketing, product differentiation is the process of distinguishing a product or offering from others, to make it more attractive to a particular target market. This involves differentiating it from competitors' products as well as a firm's own product offerings. The concept was proposed by Edward Chamberlin in his 1933 Theory of Monopolistic Competition.
Stock	The capital stock of a business entity represents the original capital paid into or invested in the business by its founders. It serves as a security for the creditors of a business since it cannot be withdrawn to the detriment of the creditors. Stock is distinct from the property and the assets of a business which may fluctuate in quantity and value.

Chapter 6. Vertical Integration

Chapter 7. Corporate Diversification

Diversification	In finance, diversification means reducing risk by investing in a variety of assets. If the asset values do not move up and down in perfect synchrony, a diversified portfolio will have less risk than the weighted average risk of its constituent assets, and often less risk than the least risky of its constituents.. Therefore, any risk-averse investor will diversify to at least some extent, with more risk-averse investors diversifying more completely than less risk-averse investors.
Product	The noun product is defined as a 'thing produced by labor or effort' or the 'result of an act or a process', and stems from the verb produce, from the Latin produce(re) '(to) lead or bring forth'. Since 1575, the word 'product' has referred to anything produced. Since 1695, the word has referred to 'thing or things produced'.
Market	A market is any one of a variety of systems, institutions, procedures, social relations and infrastructures whereby parties engage in exchange. While parties may exchange goods and services by barter, most markets rely on buyers offer their goods or services (including labor) in exchange for money (legal tender such as fiat money) from buyers. For a market to be competitive, there must be more than a single buyer or seller.
Free cash flow	In corporate finance, free cash flow is cash flow available for distribution among all the securities holders of an organization. They include equity holders, debt holders, preferred stock holders, convertible security holders, and so on. Note that the first three lines above are calculated for you on the standard Statement of Cash Flows.
Cash flow	Cash flow is the movement of cash into or out of a business, project, or financial product. (Note that 'cash' is used here in the broader sense of the term, where it includes bank deposits). It is usually measured during a specified, finite period of time.
Dominant logic	Dominant logic relates to the main means a company uses to make a profit. In essence, it is an interpretation of how a company has succeeded. It describes the cultural norms and beliefs that the company espouses.

Chapter 7. Corporate Diversification

Chapter 7. Corporate Diversification

Escalation	Escalation is the phenomenon of something getting more intense step by step, for example a quarrel, or, notably, a war between states possessing weapons of mass destruction. Compare to escalator, a device that lifts something to a higher level.
Escalation of commitment	Escalation of commitment was first described by Barry M. Staw in his 1976 paper, 'Knee deep in the big muddy: A study of escalating commitment to a chosen course of action'. More recently the term sunk cost fallacy has been used to describe the phenomenon where people justify increased investment in a decision, based on the cumulative prior investment, despite new evidence suggesting that the cost, starting today, of continuing the decision outweighs the expected benefit. Such investment may include money, time, or -- in the case of military strategy -- human lives.
Predatory pricing	In business and economics, predatory pricing is the hypothetical practice of selling a product or service at a very low price, intending to drive competitors out of the market, or create barriers to entry for potential new competitors. If competitors or potential competitors cannot sustain equal or lower prices without losing money, they go out of business or choose not to enter the business. The predatory merchant then has fewer competitors or is even a de facto monopoly, and hypothetically could then raise prices above what the market would otherwise bear.
Pricing	Pricing is the process of determining what a company will receive in exchange for its products. Pricing factors are manufacturing cost, market place, competition, market condition, and quality of product. Pricing is also a key variable in microeconomic price allocation theory.
Incentive	In economics and sociology, an incentive is any factor (financial or non-financial) that enables or motivates a particular course of action, or counts as a reason for preferring one choice to the alternatives. It is an expectation that encourages people to behave in a certain way. Since human beings are purposeful creatures, the study of incentive structures is central to the study of all economic activity (both in terms of individual decision-making and in terms of co-operation and competition within a larger institutional structure).
Globalization	Globalization describes the process by which regional economies, societies, and cultures have become integrated through a global network of political ideas through communication, transportation, and trade. The term is most closely associated with the term economic globalization: the integration of national economies into the international economy through trade, foreign direct investment, capital flows, migration, the spread of technology, and military presence. However, globalization is usually recognized as being driven by a combination of economic, technological, sociocultural, political, and biological factors.

Chapter 7. Corporate Diversification

Chapter 7. Corporate Diversification

Competitive advantage	Competitive advantage is defined as the strategic advantage one business entity has over its rival entities within its competitive industry. Achieving competitive advantage strengthens and positions a business better within the business environment. Resource-based view perspective Competitive advantage is a theory that seeks to address some of the criticisms of comparative advantage.
Stakeholder	A corporate stakeholder is a party that can affect or be affected by the actions of the business as a whole. The stakeholder concept was first used in a 1963 internal memorandum at the Stanford Research institute. It defined stakeholders as 'those groups without whose support the organization would cease to exist.' The theory was later developed and championed by R. Edward Freeman in the 1980s.
Investment	Investment is putting money into something with the expectation of profit. More specifically, investment is the commitment of money or capital to the purchase of financial instruments or other assets so as to gain profitable returns in the form of interest, dividends, or appreciation of the value of the instrument (capital gains). It is related to saving or deferring consumption. Investment is involved in many areas of the economy, such as business management and finance whether for households, firms, or governments. An investment involves the choice by an individual or an organization, such as a pension fund, after some analysis or thought, to place or lend money in a vehicle, instrument or asset, such as property, commodity, stock, bond, financial derivatives (e.g. futures or options), or the foreign asset denominated in foreign currency, that has certain level of risk and provides the possibility of generating returns over a period of time.
Political risk	Political risk is a type of risk faced by investors, corporations, and governments. It is a risk that can be understood and managed with reasoned foresight and investment. Broadly, political risk refers to the complications businesses and governments may face as a result of what are commonly referred to as political decisions--or 'any political change that alters the expected outcome and value of a given economic action by changing the probability of achieving business objectives.'.

Chapter 7. Corporate Diversification

Chapter 7. Corporate Diversification

Financial risk	Financial risk is an umbrella term for any risk associated with any form of financing. Risk may be taken as downside risk, the difference between the actual return and the expected return (when the actual return is less), or the uncertainty of that return. Risk related to an investment is often called investment risk.
Risk	Risk is the potential that a chosen action or activity (including the choice of inaction) will lead to a loss (an undesirable outcome). The notion implies that a choice having an influence on the outcome exists (or existed). Potential losses themselves may also be called 'risks'.

Chapter 7. Corporate Diversification

Chapter 8. Organizing to Implement Corporate Diversification

Diversification	In finance, diversification means reducing risk by investing in a variety of assets. If the asset values do not move up and down in perfect synchrony, a diversified portfolio will have less risk than the weighted average risk of its constituent assets, and often less risk than the least risky of its constituents.. Therefore, any risk-averse investor will diversify to at least some extent, with more risk-averse investors diversifying more completely than less risk-averse investors.
M-form	The M-form refers to an organizational structure by which the firm is separated into several semi autonomous units which are guided and controlled by (financial) targets from the centre. The 'M' stands for multidivisional.
Organizational structure	An organizational structure consists of activities such as task allocation, coordination and supervision, which are directed towards the achievement of organizational aims. It can also be considered as the viewing glass or perspective through which individuals see their organization and its environment. Many organizations have hierarchical structures, but not all.
Chief executive	Chief Executive is a term used for certain gubernatorial offices, expressing the nature of their job being analogous to a head of government. Commonly used to refer to Presidential powers given by the constitution. As Chief Executive the president can: implement policy, supervise executive branch of government, prepare executive budget for submission to congress, and appoint and remove executive officials While in most cases there is another specific style, such as (lieutenant-)governor(-general), there are a few offices formally styled Chief Executive: • in the People's Republic of China, in two special administrative regions that were under foreign colonial rule until their recent transfer of sovereignty, where the chief executive are heads of the regions and heads of government: • in Mauritius, on Rodrigues island, since 12 October 2002 autonomy was granted: • New Zealand Antarctic Territory: while not a government, the Ross Dependency is a Crown entity managed by a Board of Directors and the Chair acts as the Chief Executive.

Chapter 8. Organizing to Implement Corporate Diversification

Chapter 8. Organizing to Implement Corporate Diversification

Chief executive officer	A chief executive officer, managing director, or chief executive is the highest-ranking corporate officer (executive) or administrator in charge of total management of an organization. An individual appointed as a Chief executive officer of a corporation, company, organization, or agency reports to the board of directors. Many Chief executive officers have the title 'president and Chief executive officer'.
Chief financial officer	The chief financial officer is a corporate officer primarily responsible for managing the financial risks of the corporation. This officer is also responsible for financial planning and record-keeping, as well as financial reporting to higher management. In some sectors the Chief financial officer is also responsible for analysis of data.
Board of directors	A board of directors is a body of elected or appointed members who jointly oversee the activities of a company or organization. The body sometimes has a different name, such as board of trustees, board of governors, board of managers, or executive board. It is often simply referred to as 'the board.' A board's activities are determined by the powers, duties, and responsibilities delegated to it or conferred on it by an authority outside itself.
Director	Director refers to a rank in management. A director is a person who leads, or supervises a certain area of a company, a program, or a project. Usually companies, which use this title commonly have large numbers of people with the title of director with different categories (e.g. director of human resources).
Executive officer	An executive officer is generally a person responsible for running an organization, although the exact nature of the role varies depending on the organization. Administrative law

Chapter 8. Organizing to Implement Corporate Diversification

Chapter 8. Organizing to Implement Corporate Diversification

	While there is no clear line between executive or principal and inferior officers, principal officers are high-level officials in the executive branch of U.S. government such as department heads of independent agencies. In Humphrey's Executor v. United States, 295 U.S. 602 (1935), the Court distinguished between executive officers and quasi-legislative or quasi-judicial officers by stating that the former serve at the pleasure of the President and may be removed at his discretion.
Audit committee	In a U.S. publicly-traded company, an audit committee is an operating committee of the Board of Directors charged with oversight of financial reporting and disclosure. Committee members are drawn from members of the company's board of directors, with a Chairperson selected from among the committee members. A qualifying (cf.
President	A president is a leader of an organization, company, trade union, university, or country. Etymologically, a president is one who presides, who sits in leadership . Originally, the term referred to the presiding officer of a ceremony or meeting (i.e., chairman), but today it most commonly refers to an official.
Staff function	A staff function is a secondary business activity that supports the line functions of a business to achieve the objectives. In business management, staff functions are usually defined as all functions that are not line functions. The nature of this function is advisory.
Cost center	In business, a cost center is a division that adds to the cost of an organization, but only indirectly adds to its profit. Typical examples include research and development, marketing and customer service. Overview Companies may choose to classify business units as cost centers, profit centers, or investment centers.

Chapter 8. Organizing to Implement Corporate Diversification

Chapter 8. Organizing to Implement Corporate Diversification

Profit center	A profit center is a part of a corporation that directly adds to its profit. Overview A profit center is a section of a company treated as a separate business. Thus profits or losses for a profit center are calculated separately A profit center manager is held accountable for both revenues, and costs (expenses), and therefore, profits.
Performance management	Performance management includes activities that ensure that goals are consistently being met in an effective and efficient manner. Performance management can focus on the performance of an organization, a department, employee, or even the processes to build a product or service, as well as many other areas. Performance management as referenced on this page is a broad term coined by Dr. Aubrey Daniels in the late 1970s to describe a technology (i.e. science imbedded in applications methods) for managing both behavior and results, two critical elements of what is known as performance.
Zero-based budgeting	The term 'zero-based budgeting' is sometimes used in personal finance to describe 'zero-sum budgeting', the practice of budgeting every dollar of income received, and then adjusting some part of the budget downward for every other part that needs to be adjusted upward. Zero-based budgeting also refers to the identification of a task or tasks and then funding resources to complete the task independent of current resourcing.
Price	In ordinary usage, price is the quantity of payment or compensation given by one party to another in return for goods or services.

Chapter 8. Organizing to Implement Corporate Diversification

Chapter 8. Organizing to Implement Corporate Diversification

	In all modern economies, the overwhelming majority of prices are quoted in (and the transactions involve) units of some form of currency. Although in theory, prices could be quoted as quantities of other goods or services this sort of barter exchange is rarely seen.
Pricing	Pricing is the process of determining what a company will receive in exchange for its products. Pricing factors are manufacturing cost, market place, competition, market condition, and quality of product. Pricing is also a key variable in microeconomic price allocation theory.
Product	The noun product is defined as a 'thing produced by labor or effort' or the 'result of an act or a process', and stems from the verb produce, from the Latin produce(re) '(to) lead or bring forth'. Since 1575, the word 'product' has referred to anything produced. Since 1695, the word has referred to 'thing or things produced'.
Transfer	Transfer is a technique used in propaganda and advertising. Also known as association, this is a technique of projecting positive or negative qualities (praise or blame) of a person, entity, object, or value (an individual, group, organization, nation, patriotism, etc). to another in order to make the second more acceptable or to discredit it.
Transfer pricing	Transfer pricing refers to the setting, analysis, documentation, and adjustment of charges made between related parties for goods, services, or use of property (including intangible property). Transfer prices among components of an enterprise may be used to reflect allocation of resources among such components, or for other purposes. OECD Transfer Pricing Guidelines state, 'Transfer prices are significant for both taxpayers and tax administrations because they determine in large part the income and expenses, and therefore taxable profits, of associated enterprises in different tax jurisdictions.' Many governments have adopted transfer pricing rules that apply in determining or adjusting income taxes of domestic and multinational taxpayers.
Practice	Practice is the act of rehearsing a behavior over and over, or engaging in an activity again and again, for the purpose of improving or mastering it, as in the phrase 'practice makes perfect'. Sports teams practice to prepare for actual games. Playing a musical instrument well takes a lot of practice.

Chapter 8. Organizing to Implement Corporate Diversification

Chapter 8. Organizing to Implement Corporate Diversification

Entrepreneurship	Entrepreneurship is the act of being an entrepreneur, which can be defined as 'one who undertakes innovations, finance and business acumen in an effort to transform innovations into economic goods'. This may result in new organizations or may be part of revitalizing mature organizations in response to a perceived opportunity. The most obvious form of entrepreneurship is that of starting new businesses (referred as Startup Company); however, in recent years, the term has been extended to include social and political forms of entrepreneurial activity. When entrepreneurship is describing activities within a firm or large organization it is referred to as intra-preneurship and may include corporate venturing, when large entities spin-off organizations.
Initial public offering	An initial pubic offering , referred to simply as an 'offering' or 'flotation', is when a company (called the issuer) issues common stock or shares to the public for the first time. They are often issued by smaller, younger companies seeking capital to expand, but can also be done by large privately owned companies looking to become publicly traded. In an Initial public offering the issuer obtains the assistance of an underwriting firm, which helps determine what type of security to issue (common or preferred), best offering price and time to bring it to market.
Resource	In project management terminology, resources are required to carry out the project tasks. They can be people, equipment, facilities, funding, or anything else capable of definition (usually other than labour) required for the completion of a project activity. The lack of a resource will therefore be a constraint on the completion of the project activity.

Chapter 8. Organizing to Implement Corporate Diversification

Chapter 9. Strategic Alliances

Distribution	Product distribution is one of the four elements of the marketing mix. An organization or set of organizations (go-betweens) involved in the process of making a product or service available for use or consumption by a consumer or business user. The other three parts of the marketing mix are product, pricing, and promotion.
Joint venture	A joint venture is a business agreement in which parties agree to develop, for a finite time, a new entity and new assets by contributing equity. They both exercise control over the enterprise and consequently share revenues, expenses and assets. There are other types of companies such as Joint venture limited by guarantee, joint ventures limited by guarantee with partners holding shares.
Diversification	In finance, diversification means reducing risk by investing in a variety of assets. If the asset values do not move up and down in perfect synchrony, a diversified portfolio will have less risk than the weighted average risk of its constituent assets, and often less risk than the least risky of its constituents.. Therefore, any risk-averse investor will diversify to at least some extent, with more risk-averse investors diversifying more completely than less risk-averse investors.
Economies of scale	Economies of scale, in microeconomics, refers to the cost advantages that a business obtains due to expansion. There are factors that cause a producer's average cost per unit to fall as the scale of output is increased. 'Economies of scale' is a long run concept and refers to reductions in unit cost as the size of a facility and the usage levels of other inputs increase.
Tacit collusion	Tacit collusion occurs when cartels are illegal or overt collusion is absent. Put another way, two firms agree to play a certain strategy without explicitly saying so. Oligopolists usually try not to engage in price cutting, excessive advertising or other forms of competition.
Collusion	Collusion is an agreement between two or more persons, sometimes illegal and therefore secretive, to limit open competition by deceiving, misleading, or defrauding others of their legal rights, or to obtain an objective forbidden by law typically by defrauding or gaining an unfair advantage. It is an agreement among firms to divide the market, set prices, or limit production. It can involve 'wage fixing, kickbacks, or misrepresenting the independence of the relationship between the colluding parties'.

Chapter 9. Strategic Alliances

Chapter 9. Strategic Alliances

Investment	Investment is putting money into something with the expectation of profit. More specifically, investment is the commitment of money or capital to the purchase of financial instruments or other assets so as to gain profitable returns in the form of interest, dividends, or appreciation of the value of the instrument (capital gains). It is related to saving or deferring consumption. Investment is involved in many areas of the economy, such as business management and finance whether for households, firms, or governments. An investment involves the choice by an individual or an organization, such as a pension fund, after some analysis or thought, to place or lend money in a vehicle, instrument or asset, such as property, commodity, stock, bond, financial derivatives (e.g. futures or options), or the foreign asset denominated in foreign currency, that has certain level of risk and provides the possibility of generating returns over a period of time.
Competitive advantage	Competitive advantage is defined as the strategic advantage one business entity has over its rival entities within its competitive industry. Achieving competitive advantage strengthens and positions a business better within the business environment. Resource-based view perspective Competitive advantage is a theory that seeks to address some of the criticisms of comparative advantage.
Trust	A special trust is a business entity formed with intent to monopolize business, to restrain trade, or to fix prices. Trusts gained economic power in the U.S. in the late 19th and early 20th centuries. Some, but not all, were organized as trusts in the legal sense.

Chapter 9. Strategic Alliances